INSIDE THE WORLD OF SPORTS

INSIDE THE WORLD OF SPORTS

AUTO RACING
BASEBALL
BASKETBALL
EXTREME SPORTS
FOOTBALL
GOLF
GYMNASTICS
ICE HOCKEY
LACROSSE
SOCCER
TENNIS
TRACK & FIELD
WRESTLING

INSIDE THE WORLD OF SPORTS

SOCCER

by Andrew Luke

MC MASON CREST

Mason Crest
450 Parkway Drive, Suite D
Broomall, Pennsylvania 19008
(866) MCP-BOOK (toll free)

First printing
9 8 7 6 5 4 3 2 1

ISBN (hardback) 978-1-4222-3465-5
ISBN (series) 978-1-4222-3455-6
ISBN (ebook) 978-1-4222-8427-8

Cataloging-in-Publication Data on file with the Library of Congress

QR CODES AND LINKS TO THIRD-PARTY CONTENT

You may gain access to certain third-party content ("Third-Party Sites") by scanning and using the QR Codes that appear in this publication (the "QR Codes"). We do not operate or control in any respect any information, products, or services on such Third-Party Sites linked to by us via the QR Codes included in this publication, and we assume no responsibility for any materials you may access using the QR Codes. Your use of the QR Codes may be subject to terms, limitations, or restrictions set forth in the applicable terms of use or otherwise established by the owners of the Third-Party Sites. Our linking to such Third-Party Sites via the QR Codes does not imply an endorsement or sponsorship of such Third-Party Sites, or the information, products, or services offered on or through the Third-Party Sites, nor does it imply an endorsement or sponsorship of this publication by the owners of such Third-Party Sites.

CONTENTS

CHAPTER 1   Greatest World Cup Moments 6

CHAPTER 2   The Origin of Soccer 16

CHAPTER 3   Modern Evolution 22

CHAPTER 4   The Word Cup and Soccer Royalty 30

CHAPTER 5   U.S. Soccer 38

CHAPTER 6   Modern-Day Stars 44

CHAPTER 7   Soccer's Greatest Players 52

CHAPTER 8   The Future of Soccer 64

                   Glossary of Soccer Terms 70

                   Chronology 74

                   Further Reading, Video Credits, & Internet Resources 77

                   Index 79

KEY ICONS TO LOOK FOR:

Words to understand: These words with their easy-to-understand definitions will increase the reader's understanding of the text while building vocabulary skills.

Educational Videos: Readers can view videos by scanning our QR codes, providing them with additional educational content to supplement the text. Examples include news coverage, moments in history, speeches, iconic sports moments and much more!

Text-dependent questions: These questions send the reader back to the text for more careful attention to the evidence presented there.

Research projects: Readers are pointed toward areas of further inquiry connected to each chapter. Suggestions are provided for projects that encourage deeper research and analysis.

The winners of the FIFA World Cup association football tournament are awarded this trophy. There have been two trophies used since the first World Cup in 1930. The other is the Jules Rimet Trophy, which was replaced by the FIFA World Cup Trophy in 1974. Originally called the Victory Cup, the Jules Rimet Trophy was renamed in 1946 for the FIFA president who created the tournament. Ever since the 1974 World Cup, the FIFA World Cup Trophy, as seen here, has been the reward. This trophy is made of 18-karat gold with a malachite base. It weighs more than 13 pounds (6 kg) and stands just over 14 inches (35 cm) high. The FIFA World Cup Trophy shows two people holding up the Earth.

CHAPTER 1

GREATEST WORLD CUP MOMENTS

No sport on the entire planet comes close to rivaling the popularity of soccer. Known as football outside of the U.S. and Canada, soccer is the world's game. It is played in more than 200 countries by more than 265 million people, not counting makeshift games on city streets or in fields using rocks and tree stumps for goalposts.

The game is also the world's most popular professional sport. More than 50 million fans flock to stadiums in England, Germany, Spain, and France every season. And these four countries just scratch the surface. More than 25 countries have major professional soccer leagues, from Mexico and Turkey to South Africa and the U.A.E.

Perhaps the best illustration for American audiences can come from comparing with an event they know. The National Football League (NFL) championship game, the Super Bowl, is the most popular televised event in the U.S. More than 114 million viewers in the U.S. watched Super Bowl XLIX in February of 2015, which is a record. The broadcast also drew another 46 million viewers across the globe, for a total of about 160 million. That's a lot. Compared to soccer's biggest event, however, 160 million fails to impress.

The World Cup is a soccer tournament held every four years since 1930, featuring 32 qualifying teams from countries in six regions across the globe. In 2006, the event was held in Germany, and the final match featured the teams from Italy and France. More than 260 million people tuned in live to watch Italy claim victory. That 260 million includes verified viewers in 90 percent of the world's TV markets. It is estimated that total viewership was closer to 400 million. That is anywhere from 60 to 150 percent more viewers than watched Super Bowl XLIX.

The World Cup attracts this kind of attention because it brings together the greatest players in the world representing their nations for the global championship of the world's most popular sport. It is no surprise that over its history, the World Cup has produced some of the sport's greatest moments.

Miracle of Bern

The 1954 World Cup Final in West Germany is dubbed the "Miracle at Bern." Referring to it as a miracle conjures a biblical story: David versus Goliath. For home team West Germany, the outlook was dire going against Ferenc Puskás and mighty Hungary.

Hungary had won 32 straight games coming into the tournament. They had already beaten Germany 8-3 in the group stage and defeated the previous World Cup finalists Brazil and Uruguay to get to the final match. Germany sought to put forth a stronger showing with the world watching. That plan got off on poor footing when Puskás scored in the first six minutes. It was 2-0 after eight minutes. Germany regrouped, however, scoring two goals of their own in the next 10 minutes to tie. Buoyed by some brilliant goalkeeping, Germany withstood waves of attacks and secured the upset by scoring with six minutes left.

The Perfect Goal

After losing in the 1950 final and then in the quarterfinals in 1954, Brazil won the World Cup in 1958 and 1962 behind young superstar Edson Arantes do Nascimento, who is better known as Pelé. La Canarhino lost in the first round in 1966, however, and came into the 1970 final in Mexico looking for redemption.

The 1970 tournament featured a wide-open style of play, and the skilled Brazilians took full advantage. Nowhere was this skill level more evident than in the 86th minute of the final match against Italy. With the match already in hand at 3-1, defender Clodoaldo beat four Italians in his own half before passing to Rivelino. Rivelino passed down the left wing to Jairzinho, who crossed from the wing to the center of the box to Pelé. Pelé held the ball, waiting for the oncoming Carlos Alberto, who took the pass sprinting up from his right back position and buried it from the corner of the box.

Rossi's Hat Trick

Italy won two World Cups in the 1930s, but that 1970 loss to Carlos Alberto and Brazil was the closest they had come since. That all changed in Spain in 1982, when the Azzurri were led by 26-year-old striker Paolo Rossi.

Italy faced heavily favored Brazil in the quarterfinals, a match that Rossi won single-handedly. He opened the scoring in the fifth minute, heading in a cross for a 1-0 lead. Brazil scored to tie it at 1-1 when Rossi struck again, intercepting a pass in the Brazilian half and drilling home the goal to make it 2-1. In the second half, Brazil equalized once more, but in the 74th minute, a Brazilian defender botched the clearance of an Italian corner kick, which went right to Rossi, who volleyed it home for the hat trick and the 3-2 win. He scored three more goals in the next two games as Italy won the Cup.

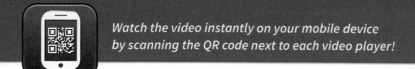
Watch the video instantly on your mobile device by scanning the QR code next to each video player!

Hand of God

The following World Cup belonged to another young striker, Argentina's Diego Maradona. In 1986, Argentina arrived in Mexico as an underdog to win the title but played well in the group stage and second round to advance to the quarterfinals against England.

The quarterfinal match was scoreless at the start of the second half when Maradona scored one of the most controversial goals in history. On a clearing attempt in his own box by English defender Steve Hodge, he mishit it, and the ball corkscrewed over to Maradona, who was running directly down the center of the area. Maradona raised his arms and jumped to head the ball, but punched it into the goal with his hand instead. The referee did not see the hand ball, and the goal counted. After the game, Maradona famously said the goal was "a little with the head of Maradona and a little with the hand of God."

Goal of the Century

In that same 1986 quarterfinal against England, Maradona scored another (this time legal) goal. He had just scored the infamous Hand of God goal when he struck again four minutes later.

Argentina led England 1-0, and the English were still in shock and enraged over the first goal. Maradona did not relent, however, picking up the ball 60 yards (55 m) from the English goal and weaving through four defenders before executing a move (a deke) that left the English keeper on the seat of his pants. Maradona calmly rolled the ball into the open goal to make it 2-0. That proved to be the dagger that eliminated England, as the match ended 2-1. Argentina was propelled to the World Cup title from there. As for the goal, a 2002 poll by the sport's governing body, Fédération Internationale de Football Association (FIFA), named the play the Goal of the Century.

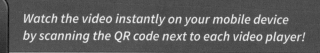

Zidane Uses His Head

Just as Maradona was the Golden Ball winner as most valuable player (MVP) in 1986, so was French superstar Zinedine Zidane at the 2006 World Cup in Germany. France advanced to the final of the tournament against Italy, and everyone knew it would be the final match for the much-heralded Zidane, who announced his retirement before the tournament.

Zidane started the match against Italy in outstanding fashion, scoring in the seventh minute. Later in the match, however, celebration turned to shame. Marco Materazzi scored to tie the game and force extra time. In the 110th minute, Zidane and Materazzi were jogging close together. Materazzi tugged at Zidane's jersey, and they exchanged some words. Zidane jogged ahead of Materazzi, then stopped, turned, and drove the crown of his head into Materazzi's chest. Zidane received a red card and was ejected from the game. France lost the match in extra time, and Zidane's career ended in disgrace.

Chastain Wins It

The 1999 Women's World Cup was held in the United States. This was the third edition of the women's tournament, and the American women were looking to improve on their third-place finish in 1995.

The Americans started strongly, going undefeated in the group stage and outscoring opponents 13-1. They continued to play well, advancing to the final against China. A women's sports record crowd of more than 90,000 turned out to watch the final, which remained scoreless through extra time. The match was decided by a penalty kick shootout. After nine shooters had kicked, the teams were tied at 4-4 with only American Brandi Chastain left to shoot. When Chastain scored to win the match, she pulled off her jersey and fell to her knees flexing her arms. The image of Chastain in her sports bra made the cover of several magazines and is one of the most famous images in women's athletics.

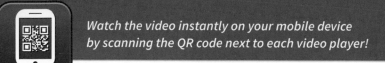

Iniesta Is Golden

Entering the 2010 World Cup in South Africa, Spain was on a roll. They won the Euro 2008 tournament, and before losing to the U.S. in June 2009, they had won a record 35 matches in a row. Spain came to South Africa confident and ready to play. After a stumble in the first group stage match against Switzerland, La Roja won its group and rolled through the rest of the tournament undefeated, all the way to the final match against Holland.

The final was tight throughout, remaining scoreless into extra time. Finally, with Spain attacking in the 116th minute, a blocked cross fell at the feet of Cesc Fabregas at the top of the penalty area. He spotted Andres Iniesta standing open on the right. Iniesta controlled the pass with one touch and then volleyed it home with the second touch for the sudden death World Cup winning goal.

Kemari is an ancient Japanese game where players use any body part other than their hands to keep a ball in the air.

 Words to Understand:

kemari: a ball game that was popular in Japan during the Heian Period

honing: to make more acute or effective; improve; perfect

barbarous: uncivilized; wild; savage; crude

CHAPTER 2

THE ORIGIN OF SOCCER

Who can lay claim to inventing the beautiful game? Many nations have some version of an origin story, but experts believe the first foundations of the game that would become soccer were laid 4,000 years ago in China. The original version was called tsu-chu and played with a ball stuffed with cork and hair that was kicked back and forth. Around 700 BC, a similar game called **kemari** emerged in Japan. In North Africa, the Berbers used the head from an animal sacrifice as a ball, competing for the right to bury the head.

THE GAME SPREADS

The Greeks brought the game to Europe, and the Romans learned it from them. The game was popular with Roman soldiers, who spread it to every corner of the empire. By 40 BC, the Romans had established trading and diplomatic links with Britain, exporting the game there. It proved especially popular in the British Isles, where citizens of all classes took to the sport.

The English made the game their own, **honing** and developing it through the centuries. In 1175, an English monk wrote about a game called ludus pilae, played with animal heads, then bladders, and eventually an animal-skin ball. Games involved all the men of the town playing against all the men from the neighboring town and often ended in violence. The game had few rules, allowed unlimited players, and was wildly popular with the masses.

A VIOLENT PASTIME

Much of the game's popularity stemmed from the low barrier of entry to play. All that was needed was an object to kick, some willing players, and space to play. It was not only for the rich. It was also not for the faint of heart. Games were physically brutal. The sport became known in English as football rather than by the Latin ludus pilae. The games left players with broken necks and legs and constantly was filled with brawls that led to a public outcry against the sport. Writers of the day described it as "beastly fury," "extreme violence," or sometimes "murder."

Society leaders took a stand against the game's brutality, and eventually King Edward II banned football throughout England in 1314. King Edward III reinforced the ban among his soldiers, who preferred playing the game rather than practicing their archery during a war with France. Soldiers caught playing football or what he deemed to be other "idle games" would be imprisoned.

THE FORBIDDEN SPORT

In 1389, the ban was expanded by King Richard II specifically to include tennis as well as football. In Scotland in 1457, King James III ordered the ban of both football and golf. The next century gave no further opportunity for football to thrive as Queen Elizabeth I declared that "no football be played within the city of London upon pain of imprisonment."

Edicts, bans, and declarations aside, the game could not be policed in every nook and cranny. It flourished in the rural areas of England, where rivalries sprung up between neighboring villages, which played for area championships. Rules began to evolve, with variations from region to region. Instead of starting between two villages and trying to kick the ball into the opposing village, goals were defined, and the distance between them was reduced to half a mile.

THE BEAUTIFUL GAME EMERGES

By the 1800s, the game had evolved from a brutal and **barbarous** affair to one with defined rules, although there still were regional variations. Schools embraced the sport as a central form of competition with other schools. Some school competitions disallowed the use of hands to advance the ball. Other schools, however, did allow players to pick up the ball and run with it. From these two particular variations, two forms of football emerged. One would develop into rugby, and the other maintained the name football and developed into the game we now know.

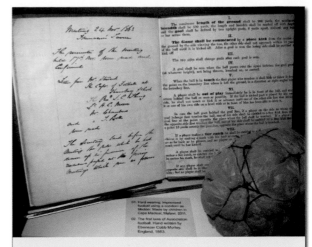

The original Laws of the Game at the National Football Museum in Manchester, England.

By the mid-1800s, more and more organization had crept into the sport, until a group from Cambridge University finally compiled a set of rules in 1848. These rules set out to abolish the common practice of kicking the opponent in the shins, known as hacking. The rules were designed to promote skill and punish violence.

By 1863, there were several football clubs that followed the Cambridge rules. Eleven of them met that year to form the London Football Association, which established rules that stated, "Neither tripping nor hacking shall be allowed, and no player shall use his hands to hold or push an adversary." These new rules were issued on December 8, 1963, which is considered to be the founding date of the modern-day sport of football. In the United States, of course, it is commonly called soccer.

SOCCER IS BORN

Although now used only in North America to distinguish it from American or Canadian football, the term soccer originated as slang in England. It comes from the third through fifth letters of association, as in the London Football Association, and referred to those who were playing the game under the association's rules but with er added to the end. The formal name for the game today is still Association Football.

The term soccer eventually lost its popularity in England, but it persisted in North America, especially as American football emerged and needed a name. Association Football formally became soccer in America.

A group from Cambridge University compiled the first set of formal rules for soccer in 1848.

Text-Dependent Questions:

1. Who banned football throughout England in 1314?

2. When did a group from Cambridge University finally compile a set of rules for the sport?

3. Where did the term soccer originate from?

 Research Project:

Go to your local library and check out books, search old newspapers, and peruse the Internet to find artifacts that represent the origin of soccer. Locate images and articles showing and describing the game, players, old uniforms, equipment, and so on. Share your findings by creating an online scrapbook.

CONCACAF

UEFA

AFC

CAF

CONMEBOL

O
F
C

Map of the members of FIFA according to their confederation

AFC - *Asian Football Confederation in Asia and Australia*
CAF - *Confederation of African Football in Africa*
CONCACAF - *Confederation of North, Central American, and Caribbean Association Football in North America and Central America*
CONMEBOL - *Confederación Sudamericana de Fútbol in South America*
OFC - *Oceania Football Confederation in Oceania*
UEFA - *Union of European Football Associations in Europe*

Words to Understand:

imperialism: the policy of extending the rule or authority of an empire or nation over foreign countries or of acquiring and holding colonies and dependencies

boisterous: rough and noisy; noisily jolly or rowdy; clamorous; unrestrained

relented: to soften in feeling, temper, or determination; become more mild, compassionate, or forgiving

CHAPTER  3

MODERN EVOLUTION

The first national championship took place while the sport still had amateur status. In 1872, the Challenge Cup was held in Glasgow between teams representing England and Scotland. The competition expanded rapidly and, by 1882, was a 73-team tournament.

THE FIRST PROFESSIONALS

The Scots are believed to be the first to bring professionalism to the game. The practice of paying players began in Scotland in the 1880s and soon spread throughout Great Britain. By 1888, the all-professional, 12-team Football League had formed.

As the Romans did before them, the British spread the game across the globe through their **imperialism**. By the end of the 19th century, soccer was truly a global sport. Professional leagues emerged in Germany and throughout Europe. British railway workers spread the game to Argentina in the 1860s, and the first pro league emerged there in the 1890s.

FÉDÉRATION INTERNATIONALE DE FOOTBALL ASSOCIATION

With world demand for the sport growing, so did the need for it to be better organized. In 1904, seven countries sent representatives to Paris to form a governing body. The founding member countries are: France, Belgium, Denmark, Holland, Spain, Sweden, and Switzerland. FIFA, as the organization is commonly known, remains the global governing body today.

THE RISE OF CLUB SOCCER

While FIFA would eventually grow and succeed at uniting soccer on an international level, professional soccer within individual countries continued to grow into the 20th century. Dozens of countries would come to form major professional leagues. Some countries have multiple leagues.

Although South America produces some of the best players and some of the world's most passionate fan bases, the top club leagues are found in Europe. The relative financial stability and economic strength of Europe allows its clubs to pay top dollar and, therefore, attracts the best players. The top leagues are found in England, Germany, Spain, and Italy.

Lionel Messi

THE ENGLISH LEAGUES

In general, most of the world's best players can be found playing in England. Players in England's Premier League earn 60 percent more on average than those in the next-highest paying league. In 2014, for example, Premier League players averaged $3.5 million per season, the highest in the world. Striker Wayne Rooney of Manchester United was the top-paid player that season, earning $24.5 million.

Rooney's United club is one of the top professional sports properties in the world. Manchester United was worth more than $2.8 billion in 2014, more than any American sports entity, including the New York Yankees or the Dallas Cowboys. Manchester United has won a record 20 English League titles. More than 350 million fans across the globe identify themselves as United supporters.

The English Premier League has a host of other prestigious clubs renowned in world club soccer, such as Chelsea, Arsenal, and five-time European Cup champions Liverpool.

England's second professional division (there are four major pro divisions) is known as the Football League Championship. Despite being a second-tier division, the Championship draws the eighth-most fans of any club league in the world, demonstrating the popularity of soccer in England.

THE BUNDESLIGA

Germany's top league, the Bundesliga, is known for its **boisterous** fan base and has the highest average attendance of any club league in the world. Borussia Dortmund perennially tops the chart for highest average attendance among German clubs.

Despite the unwavering support for Dortmund, the most successful and popular German club is Bayern Munich. Valued at more than $1.8 billion, it was the seventh-most valuable sports property in the world in 2014. The club has won five European Championships.

The average Bundesliga player made about $2.3 million per season in 2015. The top six highest-paid players were all with Bayern Munich, led by midfielder Franck Ribery at about $12.5 million per season.

THE SPANISH LEAGUE

In Spain's top league, Liga BBVA (known as La Liga), there are only two teams that make an impact outside of Spain. It is no coincidence that these are the teams with the highest salary rosters in the world, Real Madrid and FC Barcelona. These are the world's top sports properties, each club worth more than $3 billion. The average La Liga player made $1.9 million in 2014. Real's average player made about $8.3 million. Winger Cristiano Ronaldo of Real Madrid made $41 million alone. Barcelona striker Lionel Messi made $50 million.

The two clubs get a good return on their investment on the field. Real Madrid has won 10 European Championships. Barcelona has won five. As of 2015, there were 84 La Liga champions. Real had won the title 32 times and Barcelona 23 times. No other club had won more than 10.

SERIE A

Italy was once the place to play for the world's top players. The top Italian league, Serie A, was the very best in the world in the 1990s. Stars like Zinedine Zidane, Diego Maradona, and Ronaldo were lured to Italy with big dollars to play against the best competition.

Experts blame the decline from the number one to the number four league in Europe on poor management. Owners did not treat their clubs as primary business interests but rather as secondary hobbies, allowing stadiums to fall into disrepair and the fan experience at games to deteriorate. Stadium attendance lagged, and major corporate sponsors looked to the other major leagues as a result. The 2006 match-fixing scandal was the final straw for fans. Major clubs were found guilty of colluding with officials to favor their teams. Sanctions were widespread, the harshest of which stripped Juventus of two league titles and relegated them to second-tier division Serie B.

Players left in droves, and it has been a challenge for the league to regain its standing with players and fans alike. The recovery continues, however. The average salary is just over $2 million per season. Now back in Serie A, Juventus can still boast world-class players like Andrea Pirlo, Arturo Vidal, and goalkeeper Gianluigi Buffon and is dominating the league once again. Other former powerhouses like AC Milan and Internazionale, however, are still struggling to recapture past glory.

THE BEST OF THE REST

Some of Europe's other top clubs exist outside of the top four leagues. Examples include Paris Saint-Germain in the French league, four-time European champion Ajax in the Dutch Eredivisie, and Celtic in the Scottish league. In Portugal, Benfica and Porto have seen recent success revitalize the Primeira Liga there.

CLUBS ON THE WORLD STAGE

The FIFA Club World Cup has been contested annually since 2005 between the representatives of the world's six regional qualifying zones, which are Europe, South America, North and Central America, Africa, Asia, and Oceania. Winners have come only from either Europe or South America.

Andrea Pirlo

The winners from Europe all have familiar names: Barcelona, Real Madrid, Bayern Munich, AC Milan, Internazionale, and Manchester United. The other winners are all from South America.

SOUTH AMERICAN CLUB SOCCER

Brazil's Serie A and Argentina's Primera Division are the best leagues in South America, and both are considered to be among the top 10 in the world.

In Argentina, River Plate and Buenos Aires rivals Boca Juniors are the top clubs in terms of popularity and success. River has won 36 league titles and two Copa Libertadores, the regional championship for South America. Boca has claimed 30 league titles and six Copa Libertadores, which is second only to one-time Buenos Aires powerhouse Independiente.

In Brazil, two-time FIFA Club World Cup champions Corinthians and Flamengo are the biggest clubs. Brazil is arguably the world's top soccer nation, consistently producing top-tier players year after year. But by far the biggest contribution to the game to come out of Brazil is Pelé.

PELÉ

Pelé is regarded widely to be the best soccer player in history. Pelé was born about 200 miles from Sao Paulo in southeastern Brazil. Soccer was in his genes as his father was a professional player. He received the name Pelé in school, but the exact origin of it is beyond his recall.

Pelé

Learning the game from his father, he played in amateur leagues around Sao Paulo, eventually landing with the Bauru Athletic Club Juniors. After he led Bauru to three straight youth championships, his coach took Pelé to Santos to try out with FC Santos, a professional team in Brazil's top division. Santos Manager Luis Perez signed Pelé immediately. On September 7, 1956, he scored in his very first pro match.

Pelé rocketed to superstardom in Brazil. In 1957, he not only led Santos in scoring but the entire league as well.

In 1962, he led Santos to a Copa Libertadores victory. In 1963, Santos defended its title thanks to the magic of Pelé. In the first leg against Botafogo, he scored in the final minute to gain a crucial 1-1 draw. He was then spectacular in the next leg, scoring a hat trick in a 4-0 victory. In the final against Boca Juniors, Santos won the first leg in Argentina 3-2 and then held on to win the Copa on home soil with another goal from Pelé.

He played his entire 19-year Brazilian club career with Santos and is its all-time leading scorer with more than 600 domestic club goals. He played his last three seasons in New York with the Cosmos of the North American Soccer League.

It was on the world stage where Pelé made his mark on the game. He played 92 matches for Brazil over the years, scoring 77 goals. Many of these came on soccer's biggest stage, the World Cup.

Pelé burst onto the World Cup scene in Sweden in 1958. The youngest player in the tournament at just 17, he scored the only goal of the quarterfinal match against Wales to advance Brazil to the semifinal against France. In that match, the legend was born. Pelé scored three goals to lead his team to a 5-2 win and a place in the final match against home team Sweden. Pelé scored twice more in the final match as Brazil repeated the 5-2 score from the previous round to win its first World Cup. Pelé had scored six goals in just four matches.

Pele's stamp

In 1962, the World Cup was held in Chile, but after scoring a goal in Brazil's first match, Pelé suffered an injury that kept him out the rest of the tournament, which Brazil went on to win.

By 1966, Pelé was by far the most famous player in the world, and teams came into the World Cup in England determined not to let Pelé beat them. They fouled him hard and often. Once again he scored in the first match against Bulgaria. And once again, he was injured on a foul and had to miss the next match against Hungary, which Brazil lost. He returned for the third match against Portugal but was once again fouled viciously throughout the game, and Brazil was eliminated with a loss.

After 1966, Pelé vowed never to play another World Cup match but **relented** the year before the 1970 competition in Mexico. At nearly 30, Pelé was a veteran on the Brazil team, which saw many old stars like Garrincha and Djalma Santos retire and new ones like Jairzinho, Rivelino, and Carlos Alberto come in. Soccer historians say the 1970 Brazil World Cup squad is the best ever assembled. They rolled through the group stage undefeated and were barely challenged on the way to another World Cup tournament victory, beating Italy 4-1 in the final. Pelé scored four goals in the tournament, including one in the final, and received the Golden Ball as the tournament MVP.

Pelé retired from international competition the following year, but his mark on the international game is indelible. As his career began, and again as it ended, he shone on soccer's biggest stage at the World Cup.

Brazil's 1970 World Cup team

Text-Dependent Questions:

1. The practice of paying players began in what country in the 1880s?

2. In Spain's top league, Liga BBVA (known as La Liga), what are the names of the only two teams that make an impact outside of Spain?

3. Who is regarded widely to be the best soccer player in history?

Research Project:

Do some investigating online to find the current salaries of players in different positions and on different teams today. Then look back at how the salaries for various positions progressed over the years since the first players in Scotland were paid to play in the 1880s.

Official poster of the 1930 World Cup

 Words to Understand:

harbored: to keep or hold in the mind; maintain; entertain

pedigree: an ancestral line; line of descent; lineage; ancestry

tactical: of or relating to a maneuver or plan of action designed as an expedient toward gaining a desired end or temporary advantage

CHAPTER

THE WORLD CUP AND SOCCER ROYALTY

Competitive international soccer began with a match between England and Scotland in 1872. From there, the need to compete against other nations began to grow. Uruguay and Argentina began their historic rivalry with a match in 1902. As the sport gained popularity, it became more accepted. Soccer was included in the 1900 and 1904 Olympic Games as a demonstration sport. It became an official sport in 1908, and despite being an amateur competition, the Olympic experience would represent soccer on the international stage for the next two decades.

PROFESSIONALS ON THE WORLD STAGE

There were a couple of attempts at a professional international tournament, both in Turin, Italy, in 1908 and 1909. One significant difference was that the participating countries were represented by professional club teams rather than by the best players from those countries.

FIFA began running the Olympic tournament in 1914 and was content to have the amateur contest as the premier international event for the sport through the 1928 games. In 1928, however, due to the decision that the 1932 Olympic Games in Los Angeles would not include soccer because Americans would not attend the matches, FIFA finally planned to host its own tournament.

THE FIFA WORLD CUP

The South American nation of Uruguay had won both the 1924 and 1928 Olympics and was celebrating 100 years of independence in 1930. Therefore, FIFA President Jules Rimet chose Uruguay as the host nation for the first tournament dubbed the World Cup.

In 1930, just 13 teams, including seven from South America, four from Europe, and two from North America, represented the world. Host nation Uruguay won the tournament with a 4-2 victory over Argentina.

GROWING PAINS

Many European nations claimed economic hardship as the reason they chose not to participate in the first World Cup tournament. Uruguay **harbored** such resentment over what they perceived as a snub that they refused to participate in the tournament again until 1950.

Italy hosted and won the 1934 tournament as well as the 1938 tournament in France. Some South American teams boycotted, and England refused to participate in these early World Cups.

THE WORLD UNITES

World War II caused the cancelation of the event until 1950 when it was held in Brazil. For the first time, England entered a team in qualifying and was represented at the tournament after years of refusing to be included in FIFA. Uruguay returned as well and won, but several Eastern European teams boycotted, and Germany was banned.

In 1954 in Switzerland, the tournament was held without a boycott and with representation through qualifying of teams from Europe, the Americas, and Asia. Three nations made their World Cup debuts. Germany's ban was lifted, and they responded by winning. The tournament had come a long way. The 1954 event was the first to be televised, indicating that the World Cup had finally found its footing as a premier global sporting event.

Qualifying round for 2015 FIFA Women's World Cup

FIFA WOMEN'S WORLD CUP

Since 1991, the women's game has had its own tournament, held every four years since the first event in 1991 in China. The first six events had only 12 teams, but as the women's game grew around the world, it expanded eventually to include 24 teams by 2015.

The United States women have been the dominant team on the world stage. They have finished no worse than third in every World Cup, winning the tournament three times.

Three women have been named FIFA World Player of the Year on more than one occasion since the inaugural award in 2001: Brazil's Marta (5 wins), Germany's Birgit Prinz (three wins), and Mia Hamm of the U.S. Marta is also the leading goal scorer in women's World Cup history, passing Prinz at the 2015 event in Canada.

THE CREAM RISES

The FIFA World Cup has been held without interruption every fourth year since 1950, for a total of 20 events through 2014. In the 20 events, there have been only eight nations to win. Three countries have managed to win one time each, England in 1966, France in 1998, and Spain in 2010. Uruguay had its victories in 1930 and 1950. The remaining four countries have all won at least two World Cups and finished in the top two (winner or runner-up) at least five times. These countries are considered to be international soccer royalty.

BRAZIL

Brazil is considered to be the greatest soccer-playing nation in the world. The country's **pedigree** in the World Cup is the main reason for this. Brazil has competed in every World Cup competition, winning the tournament a record five times, in 1958, 1962, 1970, 1994, and 2002. They were also runners-up in 1950 and 1998.

Birgit Prinz

Brazil has produced some of the greatest soccer players of all time. Many of them were members of the 1970 championship team, widely considered to be the best team of all time. It included not only history's greatest player in Pelé but also the likes of Jairzinho, Carlos Alberto, Rivelino, and Tostão.

Brazil's legacy of producing superstar players goes back to the 1930s, with Domingos Da Guia and Leonidas Da Silva. The next generation of Brazilian greats brought the nation its first World Cup win in 1958, with stars like Djalma Santos, Garrincha, Nilton Santos, and Didi.

Ronaldinho

Into the end of the 20th century, the world's soccer factory produced more greats, with players like Zico, Bebeto, Cafu, and Falcao and 1994 World Cup champions Romario and Ronaldo, one of the greatest strikers of all time.

In this century, Brazil has been led by superstars like Rivaldo, Ronaldinho, Roberto Carlos, and Neymar.

Pelé, Ronaldo, Romario, Zico, and Neymar are

examples of Brazilian greats who are known by single names. The tradition of using just one name dates back to the days when Brazil was a Portuguese colony. In Portuguese, children usually are given four names. Neymar, for example, is really Neymar da Silva Santos Júnior. Given these lengthy names, from childhood, Brazilians pick up short forms or nicknames and oftentimes carry these names into adulthood. Brazil's is a culture that celebrates individuality, and the use of these names has long been a reflection of that on the national soccer teams.

GERMANY

Germany's soccer teams are not known for embracing individuality. Rather, they are the model of team efficiency and precision. Words like "organized," "well arranged," and "calm" have long been used to describe German play. In the early 2000s, there was a movement to put more excitement into the German game, but when the more entertaining games produced less successful results, this new style was abandoned.

German fans were used to winning soccer teams. Supreme **tactical** play resulted in World Cup wins in 1954, 1974, and 1990. So after falling short of victory by finishing in the top three in 2002, 2006, and 2010, manager Joachim Low went back to basics for the 2014 event. The Germans stifled the opposition, allowing only four goals in seven matches on the way to claiming the trophy. By the way, they also scored 18 goals.

Whereas German players are not known for being flashy, some of them are still among the best ever to play the game. At the top of that list is the greatest defender of all time, Franz Beckenbauer, captain of the 1974 World Cup champions and manager of the 1990 World Cup champions. Beckenbauer is one of the honorary all-time captains of the German team. The others are 1954 World Cup champion captain Fritz Walter, 1990 World Cup champion captain Lothar Matthäus, and Uwe Seeler.

Other star German players include Gerd Muller, Jurgen Klinsmann, Karl Heinz Rummenigge, and goalkeepers Sepp Maier and Oliver Kahn. Among the great German goal scorers are all-time leader Miroslav Klose, Rudi Voller, Lucas Podolski, and Michael Ballack.

ITALY

Like Germany, Italy is best known for its defensive play. In fact, comparing the two nations, the Italians are historically much less offensively minded. In the great history of Italian soccer, the leading scorer in international play is Luigi Riva, who scored 35 goals in the 1960s and 1970s. That total would not even be in the top 10 in German history. Klose scored 71 goals in his international career to lead Germany.

Paolo Maldini

The Italians, however, have used their low-scoring, defensive style to great effect over the decades. The Italians won two of their four World Cups in the 1930s, allowing three goals in the 1934 tournament and five in 1938. Those Italian teams were led by the legendary Giuseppe Meazza, who scored 33 goals in just 53 appearances for the national team.

The player who best exemplified the style of Italian football is defender Paolo Maldini, often rated behind only Beckenbauer as the greatest defender of all time. Playing through the turn of this century, Maldini was the captain of Italy for a team record 74 of his 126 appearances for the Azzurri.

Italy's other defensive legend is Maldini's teammate from 1988 to 1994, Franco Baresi. The center back had world-class vision and was an unfailingly consistent distributor of the ball from the back line. Despite being a defender, he was runner-up for the Ballon D'Or as best player in the world in 1989. Countryman and 2006 World Cup champion Fabbio Cannavaro is one of only three defenders to win the award.

Other Italian legends include 1982 World Cup hero and champion Paolo Rossi, Roberto Baggio, Giacinto Facchetti, Silvio Piola, Alessandro Del Piero, and goalkeepers Gianluigi Buffon and Dino Zoff.

ARGENTINA

Two of the most explosive players in history hail from the other South American soccer powerhouse, Argentina. Diego Maradona and Lionel Messi excelled on the national stage. Messi may go down as the leading goal scorer in Argentina's history as he has terrorized defenders with his magical ability to control the ball and shift direction. He led Argentina to a second-place finish at the 2014 World Cup. Maradona led the team to a runner-up finish in 1990 but is most famous for the 1986 World Cup, where he was unanimously voted MVP of the tournament as he led his country to victory, with five goals and five assists of his country's 14-goal tournament total.

Maradona's teammate on that 1986 team, Daniel Passarella, was also on Argentina's other World Cup-winning team in 1978, the only player to appear on both and one of the top 10 goal scorers in the country's history. Mario Kempes, who was top scorer and MVP of the tournament, led that victorious 1978 team.

Lionel Messi

Gabriel Batistuta was one of the most productive goal scorers for Argentina, scoring 56 times in just 78 appearances from 1991 to 2002. Other Argentine greats include Hernan Crespo, Ubaldo Fillol, and Roberto Ayala.

Text-Dependent Questions:

1. FIFA President Jules Rimet chose what country as the host nation for the first tournament dubbed the World Cup?

2. What country is considered to be the greatest soccer-playing nation in the world?

3. Who led Argentina to a second-place finish at the 2014 World Cup and may go down as the leading goal scorer in Argentina's history?

Research Project:

Find videos of past World Cup games over the years and watch some of the best history making moments that were caught on tape. Write about your favorite World Cup moment.

First U.S. national soccer team

Words to Understand:

prominence: the state of being important, well-known, or noticeable: the state of being prominent

influx: the arrival of a large number of people

viable: capable of succeeding

CHAPTER  5

U.S. SOCCER

While the World Cup is the most popular sporting event on the planet, America remains the most significant holdout against soccer's spell. To understand why the game has been resisted in the U.S., it is necessary to go back to the very beginning, before there even was a United States.

COLONIAL CONFLICT

In Boston in 1657, citizens complained to city officials that football players had injured them in the street. A law was passed that fined "anyone participating in such an endeavor."

Through the next century and a half, the game persisted around the country and even in Boston. At Harvard in 1827, students played the first game in what became the Bloody Monday tradition, a game between the freshman and sophomore classes. The name of the tradition stems from the fact that the game always ended in a terrible brawl, and it eventually was banned altogether.

AMERICAN FOOTBALL RULES

Harvard eventually would play another role in the history of soccer's evolution. The first soccer match as we recognize the game today was played between Princeton and Rutgers in 1869. At Harvard, however, players decided they could improve on this version of the game and devised a modified form known as the Boston Game, which allowed players to pick up the ball and run with it. They believed this version of the game to be so superior that they refused to attend a convention in 1873 to draft rules for collegiate soccer. The Boston Game eventually would evolve into American football.

AMERICAN SOCCER STRUGGLES

American soccer continued to evolve, and in 1913 the United States Football Association was formed. In 1921, the first professional league, the American Soccer League, was formed. It failed to gain sufficient attention and folded in 1933.

Americans were much more interested in baseball, which came of age as a pro game at the turn of the century, and tackle football, which was beginning to gain professional **prominence** in the late 1920s. One big issue was soccer's long history of violence on the field and in the stands. Baseball in its infancy had been plagued by unruly fans and players fighting but managed to clean up its act under the leadership of Ban Johnson. But in soccer, the brawling fans and players, and pre- and postgame rioting, were practically a tradition, and the American sports fans stayed away.

THE WORLD CUP

The sport got a boost from the very first World Cup tournament, held in Uruguay in 1930. The Americans, led by goalkeeper Jimmy Douglas, Billy Gonsalves, and Bert Patenaude, won both of their group stage matches with 3-0 shutouts of Belgium and then Paraguay. Patenaude had the first hat trick in World Cup history in the second game. Although the U.S. was beaten badly by Argentina in the semifinal, 6-0, it is to date the best showing ever for an American team at the World Cup.

The Americans also qualified for the 1934 World Cup but lost 7-1 in the first round. They qualified again in 1950 but lost in the group stage. The U.S. would not qualify again for 40 years.

THE NASL

After the American Soccer League folded, the next serious attempt to organize a pro league came in 1969, when two fledgling leagues that both started the previous year merged to form the North American Soccer League (NASL).

Things started promisingly for the new 17-team league, which landed a television contract for its first season. That season was disastrous right out of the gate, however, and a dozen teams folded. The league proceeded more cautiously after that, building stronger franchises more slowly, adding three teams in 1971, eight more in 1974, and five in 1975 to get up to 20 total. It was in that peak year of 1975 that Pelé joined the league with the New York Cosmos. Although he was in the twilight of his career, attendance was triple the usual turnout, and 10 million people watched the games on U.S. television.

Despite the **influx** of other aging foreign stars such as Johan Cruyff and Franz Beckenbauer, attendance peaked by 1980, and the league folded in 1984.

MAJOR LEAGUE SOCCER

When the U.S. was chosen to host the 1994 World Cup, the necessity to form another pro league was attached to the deal. Formed in 1993, Major League Soccer (MLS) began play in 1996 with 10 teams. Like any new league, it struggled financially in the early years. The league is run as a single entity, not as a group of franchises. It lost $250 million in the first five years and another $100 million by 2004.

Things started to change in 2002, when the U.S. made a decent run in the World Cup, losing in the quarterfinals in South Korea and putting the game on the map back home.

That year, the 2002 MLS Cup, the league championship game, drew more than 60,000 fans. Then between 2005 and 2007, the league added three teams. In 2007, the LA Galaxy signed English player and worldwide superstar David Beckham, which gave a huge boost to its credibility.

Since Beckham's arrival, the league has continued to expand and sign international stars like Frank Lampard, Thierry Henry, and Kaka. By 2018, the league expected to have 24 teams, with most of them turning a profit at the gate. In 2014, the average attendance for MLS team games was about 19,000 fans, up 40 percent from its lowest point in 2000. The Seattle Sounders averaged well over 40,000 fans per game.

For the first time in history, professional soccer is a **viable** entity in the United States. It will likely never rival what the sport is in Europe. Some American stars like Clint Dempsey and Michael Bradley play in the MLS, but the top American players, like goalkeeper Tim Howard and defender John Brooks, play in Europe, and there is one primary reason—European leagues generate the money to pay the game's biggest stars.

Game between New York City Football Club and Orlando City SC at Yankee Stadium

David Beckham

42

Text-Dependent Questions:

1. The first soccer match as we recognize the game today was played between which two university teams?

2. How many teams were a part of the North American Soccer League by 1975?

3. In 2007, the LA Galaxy signed which English player and worldwide superstar, giving Major League Soccer a huge boost to its credibility?

Research Project:

Research the average career length of professional soccer players from various countries and compare the shortest and longest careers. Do certain countries breed players with longer careers? If so, why do you think that is? Create a digital presentation to share this information with your class.

Lionel Messi

Words to Understand:

diminutive: something that is small

touchline: the boundaries on the sides of the field

dominant: more important, powerful, or successful than most or all others

CHAPTER

MODERN-DAY STARS

Soccer is a game of strategy. Teams bide their time, being careful not to make critical mistakes while waiting for the right opportunity to attack. And when attacks are successful, these are the moments that fans remember. That's why the strikers like England's Wayne Rooney and the men up front who score the goals are the sport's biggest stars and get the most attention.

THE STRIKERS

In 2015, Argentina's Lionel Messi was considered widely to be the best player in the world and many say one of the best strikers in history.

The **diminutive** Messi stands just 5'6" (1.7 m) but proves that soccer is not a sport that requires size to be a standout. He joined Barcelona in Spain's La Liga in 2005. He was named FIFA's best player in the world from 2009 to 2012. Messi is the all-time leading goal scorer in both Barcelona and La Liga history. He also set the La Liga and European season records for goals in a season in 2011–2012.

Messi's Barcelona teammate, Luis Suárez of Uruguay, joined the club in 2014 after four brilliant years with Liverpool in the English Premiership. For the 2013–2014 season, he led the Premier League with 31 goals and was named Footballer of the Year in England. He is the first non-European to win the award. He also was named Dutch Footballer of the Year in 2010 while with Ajax of the Eredivisie in The Netherlands.

For the Uruguay national team, Suárez is the all-time leading goal scorer. He led the team to the Copa America Championship in 2011.

Zlatan Ibrahimović also played with both Ajax and Barcelona. The Swedish star has made several stops in his European club career, the most successful of which came in Italy's Serie A from 2004 to 2009. He led Internazionale to three straight Serie A Championships from 2006 to 2009, leading the league in goals scored in that third season. Ibrahimović spent most of his career with French club Paris Saint-Germain, where he scored more than 100 goals.

Ibrahimović is the all-time leading goal scorer for Sweden. In 2014, the Swedish media named him the second-greatest Swedish sportsperson ever, behind tennis legend Bjorn Borg.

Cristiano Ronaldo

Lionel Messi

Luis Suárez

THE WINGERS

The art of the cross in soccer is one that is difficult to master. A 20 percent success rate would be a lot to ask of the most skillful player kicking the ball from the **touchline** into the box, often at a full sprint. Players like France's Franck Ribery are among the best in the game. These men are adept in putting the ball into the net themselves as well.

There may be none better today, and perhaps ever, from the outside than Portugal's Cristiano Ronaldo. Ronaldo signed with Manchester United as an 18-year-old in 2003. He led United to the 2004 FA Cup and three straight league championships from 2006 to 2009. In 2008, he was named FIFA World Player of the Year while leading United to Champions League and FIFA Club World Cup titles.

He signed with Real Madrid in 2009, winning consecutive Ballon d'Or awards in 2013 and 2014. He led Real to Champions League and Club World Cup titles in 2014.

Ronaldo's biggest rival on the wing is Brazil's Neymar, who plays at the other La Liga powerhouse, Barcelona. Neymar came to Barcelona after breaking in with Santos in Brazil in 2009. He led Santos to the Copa Libertadores in 2011. In 2013, Barcelona paid a transfer fee of more than $64 million for Neymar's rights. In 2014–2015 he helped Barcelona to a La Liga Championship with 22 goals.

On the international pitch, Neymar has scored 43 goals in 62 appearances for his country. He scored 15 goals in just 14 games in 2014, including four in the World Cup.

Arjen Robben of Holland is a veteran of World Cup play dating back to 2006. The Dutch finished second and third respectively in 2010 and 2014, and in both tournaments he was nominated for the MVP.

Robben's club career started in his home country with Groningen and then PSV. He helped lead PSV to the league title in 2003, winning Dutch Football Talent of the Year. He played with Chelsea from 2004 to 2007, winning two league titles and an FA Cup. He also won a league title with Real Madrid in 2008 and a Champions League title with Bayern Munich in 2013.

France's Franck Ribery

Cristiano Ronaldo

Arjen Robben

THE PLAYMAKERS

Without someone talented to distribute the ball, strikers would be much less effective. Of course, many strikers are adept at making brilliant individual runs, but attacks are more successful when there is someone like Yaya Toure, Luca Modric, or Xavi Hernandez to set the table.

Belgium's Eden Hazard is the best table setter in the game. Playing midfield for Chelsea in the English Premiership since coming over from the French league in 2012, Hazard has grown into a **dominant** passer. No Premier League player attempted or received more passes in the danger zone (from the goal mouth to the top of the 18-yard box) in 2014–2015 than Hazard. While he may not have actually scored the goal or record the assist, much of Chelsea's attack in 2014–2015 was keyed from a Hazard run.

He was named the Football Writer's Association Footballer of the Year in 2015 while leading Chelsea to the league title.

Angel Di Maria of Argentina ranks next to Hazard in terms of Premiership playmaking. The midfielder started his club career in Argentina in 2005 before coming to Europe with Benfica, taking them to the Primeira Liga title in 2009–2010.

He transferred to Real Madrid in 2010 and helped the club to a league title in 2011–2012 and a Champions League title in 2014, where he was named Man of the Match in the final. He transferred to Manchester United in August 2014 for a British record $93 million.

Internationally, he was nominated for tournament MVP in the 2014 World Cup, where Argentina was runner-up.

Andres Iniesta is a World Cup champion, having scored the tournament-winning goal for his native Spain in 2010. He was named Man of the Match in the final and was nominated for tournament MVP.

Angel Di Maria   *Eden Hazard*

In club play, Iniesta represents FC Barcelona, the club he has played for since his career started in 2002. In his time with Barcelona, the team has won seven league titles, three Champions League titles, and two FIFA Club World Cups. He has twice been named World's Best Playmaker, in 2012 and 2013, and was runner-up for the Ballon d'Or in 2010.

THE BACKS

Attacking and scoring goals get the glory and the attention of fans. Managers, however, are always on the lookout for a great defender. It is tough to lose when your side does not give up any goals, and the best defenders in the world know how to close down opponents or force them to play the ball before they are prepared to do so.

Mats Hummels is a German central defender who is a product of the Bayern Munich soccer machine, starting with their youth academy at six years old. Twelve years later, he debuted with Bayern Munich in the Bundesliga and steadily has built a reputation as a standout defender.

Thiago Silva

Hummels transferred to Borussia Dortmund in 2008. In 2010, Dortmund had the best defense in the Bundesliga and was the league champion. Dortmund also won the title the following season.

Hummels has more than 30 appearances for the German national team, including the 2014 World Cup, won by Germany with Hummels nominated for MVP.

Brazil's Thiago Silva's World Cup debut came in the 2014 tournament, where he was the team captain. He was a stabilizing force on the back line as Brazil got to the quarterfinal, where Silva scored before picking up a second yellow card, which led to his suspension for the semifinal. Without Silva and Neymar, Brazil lost 7-1 to Germany.

Mats Hummels

In club play, Silva signed with Milan in 2009 after four seasons playing B-level soccer and two more in the Brasileirão. At Milan, he won a league title in 2011. Silva transferred to Paris Saint-Germain in 2012, after which PSG won three straight league titles.

Sergio Ramos has played his entire career in his native Spain. He came up with Sevilla, playing B-level soccer there until he was promoted to La Liga in 2004. In 39 appearances with Sevilla, powerhouse Real Madrid took notice of the teenage right back and offered Sevilla a record $30 million for the 19-year-old. He has accumulated more than 300 appearances with Real, mostly as the anchor at center back.

Ramos has played in three World Cups for Spain, including the win in 2010. For Real, he has seen three league titles, a Champions League win, and a FIFA Club World Cup win.

Sergio Ramos

Gianluigi Buffon

Manuel Neuer

Petr Čech

THE KEEPERS

Even the best defenders cannot shut down the game's elite strikers on every attack. That is when the quality of a club's goalkeeper comes into play. Without stellar play between the posts from keepers like Hugo Lloris of France or Spain's Iker Casillas and Victor Valdes, great teams can appear to be merely average.

Gianluigi Buffon is a game changer. He is one of the best keepers ever to play the position. The Italian star has made more than 150 appearances for his country, including three World Cup appearances. The Italians won the 2006 World Cup behind five shutouts from Buffon. Opponents were credited with just two goals (a record), one from an own goal and one from a penalty. He was named best keeper.

He has spent his club career in Serie A with Parma and then Juventus, with whom he won eight league titles. Buffon was named World's Best Goalkeeper four times.

Manuel Neuer of Germany also has a World Cup title under his belt. In 2014, he was named the tournament's best keeper, conceding just three goals in seven matches en route to the victory.

In club play, Neuer began his career with Schalke 04 in the Bundesliga in 2006. In 2011, he transferred to Bayern Munich for nearly $25 million. Only the move of Buffon from Parma to Juventus was more expensive. He was between the posts for three straight Bayern Munich league titles from 2012 to 2015. Neuer also helped Bayern win the Champions League and the FIFA Club World Cup in 2013.

Petr Čech was a fixture at Chelsea in the English Premiership for more than a decade before transferring to bitter rival Arsenal in 2015. The Czech keeper had a glorious career at Chelsea with well over 300 appearances. He won four Premiership titles and four FA Cups. In 2011–2012, Čech led Chelsea to the Champions League title. He was named World's Best Goalkeeper in 2005.

Čech is instantly recognizable to fans for the rugby-style headgear he wears in matches. He suffered a life-threatening skull fracture in a match in 2006.

Text-Dependent Questions:

1. In 2015, which Argentinian player was considered widely to be the best player in the world and many say one of the best strikers in history?

2. Who signed with Manchester United as an 18-year-old in 2003, led the team to the 2004 FA Cup and three straight league championships from 2006 to 2009, and in 2008, was named FIFA World Player of the Year while leading United to Champions League and FIFA Club World Cup titles?

3. Which Italian goalkeeper has made more than 150 appearances for his country, including three World Cup appearances?

Research Project:

Begin to follow soccer blogs and forums to see what people are talking about and how modern-day stars are being evaluated by their audience. Participate in the conversation. Share your thoughts on your favorite soccer stars of today.

FRANZ BECKENBAUER

DJALMA SANTOS

IAN HOLLOWAY

ZINEDINE ZIDANE

ALFREDO DI STEFANO

PELÉ

BOBBY CHARLTON (RIGHT)

EUSÉBIO (RIGHT)   GORDON BANKS

PAOLO MALDINI

DIEGO MARADONA (LEFT) MICHEL PLATINI (RIGHT)

JOHAN CRUYFF (MIDDLE)

*Scan this QR code to visit the FIFA website
to learn more about Soccer's Greatest Players.*

CHAPTER 7

SOCCER'S GREATEST PLAYERS

On the field, soccer has produced some of the greatest athletes in all of sports. At the highest level, the athletes are in top physical condition, displaying world-class stamina and endurance combined with supreme coordination skill. Precision passing, ball control, dribbling, and ball striking skills are what put fans into the seats they then leap out of to cheer. It is a beautiful game, but off the field, there have been some ugly periods.

SOCCER SCANDALS

There is a lot of power and money in 21st-century soccer, and with these has also come the element of greed, which when uncovered, has resulted in scandal for the game.

Match-fixing scandals exploded in 2005 when referees in both the German second division and in the Brazil first division separately were proven to have either taken bribes to fix game outcomes (Brazil) or gambled on the games and then fixed the outcomes in their favor (Germany).

In Italy, Juventus was stripped of the 2005 and 2006 Serie A titles when it and other clubs were found to have influenced referees and referee selection.

Referees have not been the only group susceptible to bribes. In 2015, 14 former and current soccer federation officials or corporate executives, including two FIFA executive committee members, were indicted or arrested for wire fraud, racketeering, and money laundering. This case involved more than $150 million in bribes taken to secure broadcast and marketing rights.

RIOTS AND HOOLIGANISM

The specter of scandal replaced the original soccer black eye—rampant rioting. The 1980s were the heyday of hooliganism in soccer. In 1985, 39 fans were killed when a wall collapsed during a riot in the stands at the UEFA Cup final between Liverpool and Juventus in Brussels. That same year, riots at Luton and Leeds in England left millions of dollars in damage and a 14-year-old boy dead.

European countries banned English teams for five years as a result of these incidents, and the game took serious measures to clean up its act. Such incidents of violence have been very rare in this century.

THE PLAYERS PLAY

Through it all, the game on the field has endured, and fans have forgiven scandal and overcome hooligans to watch the best players the sport has to offer ply their craft.

Pelé

Eusébio

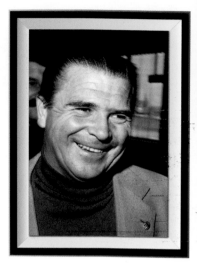

Ferenc Puskás

FORWARDS

The debate as to which forward is the best of all time begins and ends with Pelé. The Brazilian widely is considered to be the best player in history; Pelé scored a lot of goals, but it is the way that they were scored that caused his peers to rave about his talent.

"Pelé was the only footballer who surpassed the boundaries of logic."
– Legendary Dutch midfielder Johan Cruyff

"The greatest player in history was Di Stefano. I refuse to classify Pelé as a player. He was above that."
– Hungarian superstar Ferenc Puskás

And there is this exchange between British TV commentators Malcolm Allison and Pat Crerand during a Brazil match at the 1970 World Cup:

"How do you spell Pelé?"
"Easy: G-O-D."

Nearly a quarter century after Pelé played his last game for Brazil in 1971, the next generation's Brazilian superstar emerged from the streets of Rio. Ronaldo was anointed as Il Fenomeno, the Phenomenon, as a young teenager, and by age 17, he was a member of the national team.

He debuted for Brazil in 1994 and made three World Cup appearances. In his World Cup career, he won the Golden Ball, the Golden Boot, and one championship. He is also one of just four players to be named FIFA World Player of the Year three times.

The other great, one-name, Portuguese-speaking striker is not from Brazil. Eusébio hailed from Mozambique, a colony of Portugal, where he was born in 1942. He played most of his career at Benfica, Portugal's top club team, from 1960 to 1975.

Eusébio was a three-time European Cup top scorer and was named European Footballer of the Year in 1965. His breakthrough on the world stage came at the 1966 World Cup in England. Eusébio scored eight goals to win the Golden Boot while leading Portugal to a third-place finish. Four of the goals came in a match against North Korea that the Portuguese trailed 3-0.

Alfredo Di Stefano is the only player to score more European Cup goals than Eusébio. Born in Argentina, Di Stefano played his first eight pro seasons there but gained fame after his transfer to Real Madrid in 1953. He scored more than 300 goals for Real and became a Spanish citizen in 1956. He led Real to a record five straight European Cups and was European Player of the Year in 1957 and 1959. His brilliance at the club level is legendary, but unfortunately, boycotts, not qualifying, and injury prevented the legendary striker from ever playing in the World Cup.

Ferenc Puskás played only once in the World Cup, but it was a memorable appearance. His Hungarian squad was the biggest favorite in World Cup history in 1954 but lost to the Germans in the Miracle of Bern in what many consider to be the greatest upset ever. Puskás scored four times in three matches in the tournament to win the Golden Ball award for MVP.

His goal-scoring prowess was evident at the club level as well. He played in Budapest from 1943 to 1955. After refusing to return to his Hungarian club due to a revolution in that country, Puskás was suspended for two years. In 1958, he joined Real Madrid at age 31 and led them to five straight La Liga championships from 1961 to 1965.

MIDFIELDERS

Ian Holloway is a former English Premier League manager who also played midfield, mostly in the lower English divisions. He once described midfielders as piano movers, saying, "If you haven't got anyone to get the piano on the stage in the first place, the pianist would be standing there with no bloody piano to play."

Diego Maradona of Argentina was not only history's best piano mover, but he could also deliver virtuoso performances of his own. Maradona rose to prominence in Buenos Aires in the 1970s but had his greatest club success with Serie A's Napoli, leading the team to two Serie A titles.

Maradona's greatest success as a player came for his country at the World Cup, where he led Argentina to back-to-back championship game appearances in 1986 in Mexico and 1990 in Italy. He won a Golden Ball as MVP in 1986, where he dominated the tournament in leading Argentina to victory.

Michel Platini, eight-year captain of the French national team, once said of Maradona, "The things I could do with a football, he could do with an orange."

Platini may not have been Maradona's equal, but he is still one of the best to play midfield. Platini was wrapping up his brilliant career at Juventus in Serie A when Maradona arrived at rival Napoli in 1984. Platini led Juventus to two Serie A titles and a European Cup victory.

Diego Maradona

Michel Platini

Johan Cruyff

Platini was European Footballer of the Year three straight seasons from 1983 to 1985 and *World Soccer* magazine Player of the Year in 1984 and 1985.

Platini's compatriot, Zinedine Zidane, grew up in Marseilles idolizing Platini. Nineteen years after Platini played his last match for Juventus in 1987, Zizou, as Zidane was known, debuted for the club, where he also had spectacular success. Zizou was named World Player of the Year in 1998 and 2000 and again in 2003 after transferring to Real Madrid. He and Ronaldo are the only players to win the award three times.

At the 1998 World Cup in France, Zidane scored two goals in the final match against Brazil to secure his country's first and only World Cup victory. Like Platini, Zizou also went on to become France's captain.

Bobby Charlton was not captain of England's World Cup teams in its four appearances from 1958 to 1970, but he did score two of the team's most important goals in the 1966 tournament held in England. In the semifinals against Portugal, his two markers were the difference in a 2-1 win. England went on to win the tournament for the only time in its history. Charlton is England's all-time leading goal scorer.

Charlton played all but the final two of his 19 club seasons with Manchester United, where he won three league titles, an FA Cup, and a European Footballer of the Year award in 1966.

As Charlton's career was peaking in 1966, that of the Dutch grand master Johan Cruyff was just beginning. Cruyff debuted with Ajax in 1964, where he played before transferring to Barcelona in 1973. He became famous at Ajax for running the "Total Football" system, and his ability to perfectly time passes made him one of the greatest playmakers ever to take the field.

At Ajax, Cruyff's teams won three straight European Cups, and he led Barcelona to a league title in his first season there. He won European Footballer of the Year three times.

The great defender Franz Beckenbauer once called Cruyff "the best footballer Europe has produced."

DEFENDERS

Franz Beckenbauer's praise of Johan Cruyff overlooked one player in particular . . . himself. The German defender is almost unanimously considered to be the best ever to anchor a back line and, along with Pelé, Maradona, and Cruyff, is arguably the best player of all time.

Beckenbauer was known as the Kaiser and dominated games both offensively and defensively from his center back position, redefining the role of sweeper. His success began at Bayern Munich in 1964, where he led the team to four league titles and three straight European Cups in the 1970s. He also was named European Footballer of the Year in 1972 and 1976.

Beckenbauer's glory culminated in the 1974 World Cup on German soil, when he captained his German team to a tournament victory, beating Cruyff and the Dutch 2-1 in the final match. In three career World Cup appearances, Beckenbauer's teams finished no worse than third.

Nearly as unanimously as Beckenbauer is regarded as the best defender, Paolo Maldini of Italy is the next defender named as an all-time great.

Maldini played his entire career with AC Milan in Serie A, having grown up in the city where his father played for the club in the 1950s and 1960s. He led the team to seven league titles in 24 seasons, including three in a row from 1992 to 1994. Maldini's teams also won two European Cups, three Champions League titles, and a FIFA Club World Cup in 2007. Internationally, Maldini has earned the most caps as captain in Italian history.

None other than Ronaldo called Maldini "the best defender I faced over the course of my career."

There was another legendary defender on the back line of Maldini's AC Milan and Italian national teams—Franco Baresi. Baresi was Milan's center back for all but one of his 20 years with the club, and he and Maldini anchored one of the most formidable defenses in Serie A history.

In his years as captain of Milan and the Italian national team, Baresi was considered to be the best sweeper in the world. When he retired in 1997, Milan immediately retired his #6 jersey. In 1999, the club voted him as its Player of the Century.

Paolo Maldini   *Bobby Moore*   *Djalma Santos*

Another supreme center back who served as captain for his country was England's Bobby Moore. Moore led his country for nine years, from 1964 to 1973. He was the captain in 1966 when England won its only World Cup on home soil at the Old Wembley stadium. When the stadium was replaced in 2007, the new building opened with a 20-foot (6-m) tall statue of Moore out front.

Moore played most of his club career with East London's West Ham United in the top English league, where he won an FA Cup and was named England's Footballer of the Year in 1964.

In 1964, Djalma Santos was two years removed from anchoring the Brazilian defense to a second straight World Cup victory in 1962. Santos's play at right back was tough and rugged, and he had a long career supporting the team's attacking style with forays down the right side. Santos was the first player in the country's history to play more than 100 games for the national team.

Santos also played in three other World Cups for Brazil, including the 1958 final match against the home team, Sweden. That match was the only one he played in the tournament, but he was so impactful that he was still named the best right back in the World Cup.

GOALIES

For 22 seasons, Dino Zoff was a tower of strength for Italian soccer. For 16 of those seasons, he was the goalkeeper for the Italian national team. He won a European Championship for Italy in 1968, but Zoff's greatest triumph came near the end of his career in 1982, when he captained the Italians to victory in the World Cup in Spain at 40 years old.

Zoff is best remembered as the keeper for Juventus at the club level. He backed the team to six Serie A titles in his 11 seasons there in Turin. In his early years with Juventus, Zoff once went 1,142 minutes without allowing a goal.

Sixteen years after Zoff retired in 1983, Italy's next dominant goalkeeper emerged in Gianluigi Buffon. He made his first start for Italy as an injury replacement in 1997. Zoff became the Italian manager in 1998 and named Buffon to the World Cup team as the backup. Zoff promoted Buffon to starter in 2000.

Zoff left after that season, but Buffon remained to play in four more World Cups, including 2006, where he was named the Yashin award winner as best keeper of the tournament in an Italian victory.

On the club level, Buffon has been a fixture with Juventus as Zoff had been 20 years prior, winning six official league titles.

Lev Yashin is the man for whom the award for best goalkeeper in the World Cup is named. Yashin was a Russian who played for the Soviet national team for 14 seasons in the 1950s and 1960s. The Soviets never won a World Cup, but that was never Yashin's fault. He played in four World Cups from 1954 to 1966, appearing in 12 matches. In four of those, he did not allow a goal. In 1958, he was named to the World Cup all-star team, and in 1966 he led the team to a fourth-place finish.

Yashin led the Soviets to the first European Championship in 1960 and is the only keeper to be named European Player of the Year (1963).

Gordon Banks was the goalkeeper for England in that 1966 World Cup in which Yashin performed so well. Banks, playing on home soil, did not concede a goal in the first four matches of the tournament. Only a Eusébio penalty in the semifinal game eluded Banks before the final against Germany. England prevailed 4-2 in extra time, and Banks was named all-star goalkeeper for the tournament.

On the club level, Banks played most of his career with Leicester City and then Stoke City in England's top division, where he was Footballer of the Year in 1972 and FIFA Goalkeeper of the Year from 1966 to 1971.

Peter Schmeichel was also an English top-division standout at the goalkeeper position. An imposing figure at 6'3" (1.9 m) tall, he is best remembered for his time at Premier League powerhouse Manchester United, where he won five league titles, three FA Cups, and a UEFA Champions League title in 1999.

Schmeichel is from Denmark and was that country's national team keeper from 1987 to 2001, leading them to the 1992 European Championship. In a 2001 Reuters poll, Schmeichel was voted as best goalkeeper ever, a sentiment once echoed by his Manchester United manager, Sir Alex Ferguson.

Most experts, however, would not put Schmeichel ahead of Yashin, Banks, or Zoff. Yashin was named in FIFA polls as the goalkeeper on the World Team of the 20th Century. Banks himself once said of Yashin, "Everything he did was top class. He was the model for goalkeeping for the next 10 to 15 years, without a doubt."

Dino Zoff

Lev Yashin

Peter Schmeichel

Career Snapshots

Forwards

#10 FERENC PUSKÁS 1943–62

89 Caps
84 International goals
508 Club goals

#9 ALFREDO DI STÉFANO 1945–66

35 Caps
29 International goals
484 Club goals

#10 PELÉ 1956–77

92 Caps
77 International goals
680 Club goals

#10 EUSÉBIO 1957–78

64 Caps
41 International goals
423 Club goals

#9 RONALDO 1993–2011

98 Caps
62 International goals
352 Club goals

Midfielders

#9 BOBBY CHARLTON 1956–76

106 Caps
49 International goals
260 Club goals

#14 JOHAN CRUYFF 1964–84

48 Caps
33 International goals
290 Club goals

#10 MICHEL PLATINI 1972–87

72 Caps
41 International goals
312 Club goals

#10 DIEGO MARADONA 1976–97

91 Caps
34 International goals
312 Club goals

#10 ZINEDINE ZIDANE 1989–2006

108 Caps
31 International goals
125 Club goals

All the above athletes are members of the
Hall of Fame with the exception of current players

Defenders

#4 DJALMA SANTOS 1948-70

110 Caps
3 International goals
23 Club goals

#10 BOBBY MOORE 1958-73

108 Caps
2 International goals
26 Club goals

#5 FRANZ BECKENBAUER 1964-83

103 Caps
14 International goals
94 Club goals

#6 FRANCO BARESI 1977-97

81 Caps
1 International goal
33 Club goals

#3 PAOLO MALDINI 1985-2009

126 Caps
7 International goals
33 Club goals

Goalies

#1 LEV YASHIN 1950-70

75 Caps
5 League titles
1 European Championship

#1 DINO ZOFF 1961-83

112 Caps
6 League titles
1 World Cup

#1 GORDON BANKS 1958-77

73 Caps
2 Football League Cups
1 World Cup

#1 PETER SCHMEICHEL 1981-2003

129 Caps
9 League titles
1 UEFA Champions League title

#1 GIANLUIGI BUFFON 1997- Present

147 Caps
6 League titles
1 World Cup

The 2018 FIFA World Cup tournament is scheduled to take place in Russia from June 14 to July 15.

Words to Understand:

globalization: the act of extending to other or all parts of the world

berths: a place, listing, or role

ingrained: firmly fixed; deep-rooted; inveterate

CHAPTER

THE FUTURE OF SOCCER

Soccer is the biggest sport in the world, and there is little sign that this will change anytime in the near or distant future. This will be especially true as long as the sport's showpiece event continues to be the most watched in the world.

BETTER REPRESENTATION

FIFA often has taken the position that the **globalization** of the sport must be expanded to better include the nations of the Caribbean, Africa, and Asia. To do this without expanding the tournament from a 32-team format, berths likely need to be taken away from the European confederation, UEFA. UEFA gets 13 berths under the 32-team format, possibly 14 if the host nation is European.

The reason that Europe gets 40 percent of the **berths** is that it has 53 national member teams, many of which are among the best in the world. Another method that has been suggested by UEFA President Michel Platini to have more representation from other regions is to expand the field to 40 teams. He has suggested giving an additional berth to Europe, two more each for Africa and Asia, one for the Caribbean, one for South America, and a guaranteed berth for New Zealand and the Pacific Island group called Oceana.

FIFA UNREST

Platini was suspended as UEFA president in 2015 and then given an eight-year ban from the sport by a FIFA ethics committee later that same year. He was accused of accepting gifts, conflict of interest, and disloyalty to FIFA after taking a $2 million payment from former FIFA president Sepp Blatter, who resigned in June of 2015 in the wake of a massive corruption investigation of 14 FIFA officials. Blatter was later also banned for eight years. One of the central items in the corruption investigation was the awarding of bids for the sport's crown jewel, the World Cup.

FUTURE WORLD CUPS

The selection process for choosing World Cup host countries has been controversial over the years. Bidding irregularities and scandal due to accusations of bribery have plagued the process. A vote-tampering controversy during the 2006 World Cup host selection led to a change in the process, where a system that rotated host confederations was implemented for future selections. However, that system was reevaluated after Brazil submitted the only bid for the South American federation (CONMEBOL) for the 2010 event. Organizers wanted multiple bids to choose from.

For 2018 and 2022, the rotation was abandoned, and any country could bid as long as its confederation had not hosted either of the previous two events. Russia was awarded the 2018 World Cup, while the 2022 bid was won by Qatar in a very controversial vote. Therefore, the process is being reevaluated again for bidding the 2026 World Cup. In May of 2015, FIFA decided to exclude bids only from the previous host confederation.

THE WOMEN'S WORLD CUP

The 2019 FIFA Women's World Cup was awarded to France in March of 2015. France was one of only two nations to submit bids for the event, along with South Korea. Intent to submit bids for the 2023 event will be declared in 2018.

THE GAME ON THE FIELD

Soccer is known as "the beautiful game" and has remained largely unchanged for nearly a century. Over the years, however, there have been some rule changes that have made an impact. Yellow and red cards were introduced in 1970. Substitutions arrived in 1958, first just for injury, expanding to three per game in 1995. In 1992, keepers could no longer handle deliberate back passes.

POSSIBLE RULE CHANGES

These changes have added to the game. It will always have its flaws, but many are flaws that fans accept. Tweaks to the game are always being suggested, however, including the following:

- The Irish Football Association proposal for a penalty box for yellow card infractions, where offending players would have to spend 10 minutes, with their team reduced to 10 men.

- Adding a fourth substitute, allowed only in extra time—this change was proposed by FIFA and then withdrawn in 2015. Fresh legs in extra time could allow more scoring chances and a possible win before the shootout.

- Abolishing the penalty shootout. This debate goes back and forth. Is the golden goal better? Penalties were instituted in 2004 when it was deemed that teams were playing not to lose. Now teams play for the shootout.

- Implementing goal line technology. Using video review to clarify questionable goal or no-goal decisions just makes sense in a world where fans in the stadium and at home can see the replay anyway.

Aymeric Laporte

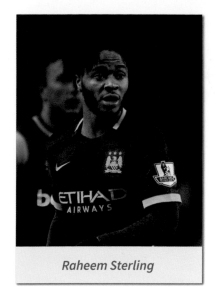

Raheem Sterling

FUTURE STARS

Which players might be adapting to new rules in the prime of their careers? World soccer certainly is filled with its share of budding young stars.

Brazilian-born center back Marquinhos already has commanded a payday of more than $40 million to transfer from Roma in Serie A to PSG in the French league. He served as captain on his county's youth teams and was an important part of the Roma defense, even as a teenager. Look for him with Brazil in the 2018 World Cup.

Frenchman Aymeric Laporte is a central defender for Athletic Bilbao in La Liga. Named to the La Liga Team of the Year after the 2013–2014 season, Laporte's strong tackling and excellent ball distribution skills have made him one of Marquinhos's peers on the back line in world soccer.

Raheem Sterling is a wide midfielder and sometimes striker for Manchester City in England's Premier League. His speed and dribbling ability are already world-class. The Jamaican-born Sterling moved to London at age seven and quickly took to the game. He won the Golden Boy award as the best European-based player under 21 in 2014.

A BEAUTIFUL FUTURE

The sport is **ingrained** into the cultures of so many nations around the globe that despite bumps and pitfalls, boys and girls continue to grow up watching and playing, ensuring the continued growth of the beautiful game.

Estadio Da Luz
Lisbon, Portugal

Estadio Monumental Antonio Vespucio Liberti
Buenos Aires, Argentina

Estadio Alberto J. Armando
Buenos Aires, Argentina

Estadio Azteca
Mexico City, Mexico

Signal Iduna Park
Dortmund, Germany

The Maracana
Rio de Janeiro

Text-Dependent Questions:

1. What is the method that has been suggested by UEFA President Michel Platini to have more representation from other regions in FIFA?

2. Name three possible rules that may change in the future.

3. Which young Brazilian-born center back already has commanded a payday of more than $40 million to transfer from Roma in Serie A to PSG in the French league?

 # Research Project:

Attend a soccer game near you. This may be a high school game, college competition or even a minor league game. Take notes on what you see from the fans, players and coaches. In your opinion, what needs to change to increase American interest in soccer? How might the proposed rule changes affect the sport?

GLOSSARY OF SOCCER TERMS

arc: the D-shaped line that spreads into the field 10 yards (9 m) from the top of the penalty area.

cap: an appearance of a country's national team. In the past, players received a cap for playing in an international competition.

card: how referees discipline players. Yellow cards are for rough or repetitive fouls. Red cards are for more violent fouls, and the player is expelled from the game. Two yellow cards by the same player in the same match equal a red card.

corner kick: a free kick taken from a corner next to the goal by the attacking team. A corner kick is called when the ball crosses the end line after touching a defender.

cross: a pass by the attacking team across the penalty area used by strikers to try to score.

defenders: players who try to keep the other team from scoring: center backs, right or left backs, and sweepers.

draw: a tie game. In league play both teams receive one point in the standings.

extra time: a 30-minute period of play added after a tie in regulation. It is used only in some tournaments, such as the World Cup. If the game is still tied after extra time, a penalty shootout decides the game.

formation: how the defenders, midfielders, and forwards are organized on the field. In a 4-4-2, for example, there are four defenders, four midfielders, and two forwards (the goalie doesn't count).

forwards: the players who play closest to the opposing goal, also called strikers. They score the most goals.

foul: called by the referee when a player breaks a rule. The fouled team gets possession and a free kick.

free kick: how the ball gets back into play after a foul. No defender can be within 10 yards (9 m) of the ball when it is kicked.

goal area: a smaller box extending 6 yards (5.5 m) from the goal inside the penalty area. This is where goal kicks are taken from.

goalkeeper: the player who stops shots at the goal. The goalkeeper can use his hands (the only player who can) but only in the penalty area.

goal kick: how play begins after the ball goes over the end line after touching an attacking player.

goal line: the line that marks each end of the field, often called the end line outside of the goal.

halfway line: the line that divides the field in half across the center between the goals.

handball: when a player (not the goalie in the penalty area) touches the ball with his hand on purpose. If the referee calls a handball, the other team gets a free kick.

midfielders: players who both defend and attack. It is their job to win the ball from the opposing team and set up scoring chances: wingers, attacking midfielders, and defensive midfielders, for example.

offside: when a player passes the ball but his teammate, while attacking, does not have two opposing defenders (usually counting the goalkeeper as one) between him and the goal line. The defending team gets a free kick when it is called. Defenses often try to catch attackers offside by moving away from their own goal.

own goal: when a defender knocks the ball into his own team's goal.

penalty: an infraction called by a referee that happens in the penalty area. The result is a free kick from the penalty spot with only the goalkeeper to beat.

penalty area: an 18-yard (16.5 m) square with one side centered on the end line. Inside the penalty area a goalkeeper may touch the ball with his hands, and a foul on the attacking team results in a penalty kick.

penalty spot: where penalty kicks are set up, a circle 12 yards (11 m) from the goal line at the center of penalty area.

shootout: when penalty kicks are used to decide a game. Each team takes five alternating shots (or more) until one teams comes out ahead.

stoppage: play time added to the end of either half to make up for time lost in substitutions or injuries.

substitutions: when one player comes in for another. The player who leaves cannot return. Usually, there are three substitutions in league play and five in friendly matches.

through ball: a pass that splits the defense to get to an onrushing attacker. This is often a pass that beats the offside trap.

throw in: how play begins after the ball goes out of bounds on the sides of the field. The player throws the ball over his head using both hands.

touchline: the boundaries on the sides of the field.

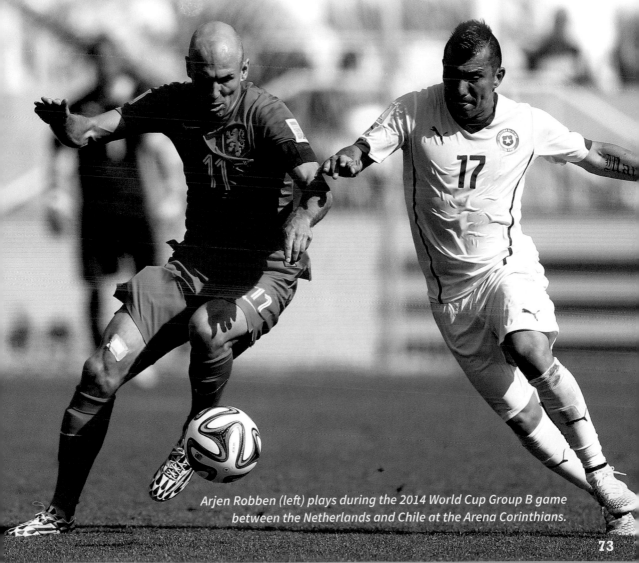

Arjen Robben (left) plays during the 2014 World Cup Group B game between the Netherlands and Chile at the Arena Corinthians.

CHRONOLOGY

AD 43–407 Roman legionnaires bring harpastum to England.

1175 The English game ludus pilae is mentioned in writing.

1572 Queen Elizabeth bans football in London.

1827 Harvard students start their Bloody Monday games.

1872 First international game is held when England plays Scotland.

1904 The Fédération Internationale de Football Association (FIFA) is organized.

1930 The first World Cup tournament is held.

1937 Nearly 150,000 people watch Scotland play England in Glasgow, the largest crowd in soccer history.

1950 The World Cup returns after two championships are cancelled due to World War II. Uruguay beats Brazil 2-1.

1955 The UEFA Champions League, now the richest sporting event in the world, is founded.

1968 The North American Soccer League (NASL) is formed.

1970 Pelé becomes the first player to win three World Cups when Brazil wins in Mexico.

1982 For the first time, the World Cup includes participants from all six inhabited continents.

1984 The NASL folds.

1991 The United States women's national team wins the inaugural Women's World Cup.

1993 Major League Soccer (MLS) is established as a professional league in the U.S. and Canada.

2000 Pelé and Argentina's Diego Maradona are named cowinners of the FIFA Player of the Century award.

2001 Real Madrid pays a world record $79 million to get French star Zinedene Zidane from Juventus.

2002 The World Cup is played outside Europe or South America for the first time, with Brazil winning a record fifth title in Japan.

2010 The World Cup is held in Africa for the first time, with Spain winning in South Africa.

2012 Lionel Messi scores a record 91 goals and wins the Ballon D'Or a record fourth time during the fourth straight year he is named as top player in the world

2015 The United States women's national team wins the Women's World Cup.

Soccer Today: In 2015-2016, world famous Spanish club FC Barcelona set a club record by going unbeaten in more than 30 matches. Barcelona is led by a trio of South Americans, including superstar Lionel Messi of Argentina, Luis Suarez of Uruguay and Neymar of Brazil. Suarez scored more than 30 goals during the streak. It was the fourth time in the 118-year club history that Barcelona has had a streak of at least 24 unbeaten games.

Manuel Neuer tries to save a shot.

FURTHER READING:

Teixeira, Thiago Jorge. *Neymar (Superstars of Soccer: Brazil)*. Broomall, PA: Mason Crest, 2013

Burshtein, Karen. *Lionel Messi: Soccer's Top Scorer (Living Legends of Sports)*. New York: Rosen Education Service, 2015

Trusdell, Brian. *Pele: Soccer Star & Ambassador (Legendary Athletes)*. Edina, MN: Abdo Publishing Company, 2014

Radnedge, Keir. *World Soccer Records 2015*. London, England: Carlton Books, 2015

INTERNET RESOURCES:

Federation Internationale de Football Association: http://www.fifa.com

Union of European Football Associations: http://www.uefa.com/

English Premier League: http://www.premierleague.com/en-gb.html

Major League Soccer: http://www.mlssoccer.com/

VIDEO CREDITS:

Miracle of Bern (pg 8) https://www.youtube.com/watch?v=bfjxgT6SDYk

The Perfect Goal (pg 9) https://www.youtube.com/watch?v=M5HbmeNKino

Rossi's Hat Trick (pg 10) https://www.youtube.com/watch?v=7FfX_0NF8T0

Hand of God (pg 11) https://www.youtube.com/watch?v=-ccNkksrfls

Goal of the Century (pg 12) https://www.youtube.com/watch?v=jk-kXwjASEE

Zidane Uses His Head (pg 13) https://www.youtube.com/watch?v=ITdPTKpGHuI

Chastain Wins It (pg 14) https://www.youtube.com/watch?v=xbdddwVP7X4

Iniesta Is Golden (pg 15) https://www.youtube.com/watch?v=QwADqit3dBE

QR CODES AND LINKS TO THIRD-PARTY CONTENT

You may gain access to certain third-party content ("Third-Party Sites") by scanning and using the QR Codes that appear in this publication (the "QR Codes"). We do not operate or control in any respect any information, products, or services on such Third-Party Sites linked to by us via the QR Codes included in this publication, and we assume no responsibility for any materials you may access using the QR Codes. Your use of the QR Codes may be subject to terms, limitations, or restrictions set forth in the applicable terms of use or otherwise established by the owners of the Third-Party Sites. Our linking to such Third-Party Sites via the QR Codes does not imply an endorsement or sponsorship of such Third-Party Sites, or the information, products, or services offered on or through the Third- Party Sites, nor does it imply an endorsement or sponsorship of this publication by the owners of such Third-Party Sites.

PICTURE CREDITS

INDEX

AC Milan, 26, 58
Ajax, 26, 46, 57
Alberto, Carlos, 9, 33
Allison, Malcolm, 54
American soccer. *See* U.S. soccer
animal heads, 17
Argentinian soccer, 11–12, *11*, 12, 26, 36.
   See also Maradona, Diego
Arsenal, 50
Athletic Bilbao, 67
Ayala, Roberto, 36

backs, 49, *49*
Baggio, Roberto, 35
Ballack, Michael, 35
balls, 17
Banks, Gordon, *52*, 60–61, 63
banning of sport, 18
Barcelona, 26, 46, 47, 57
Baresi, Franco, 35, 58, 63
Batistuta, Gabriel, 36
Bayern Munich, 25, 26, 47, 49, 50, 58
Bebeto, 33
Beckenbauer, Franz, 34, 40, *52*, 57, 58, 63
Beckham, David, *3*, 41, *42*
Benfica, 26, 55
bidding irregularities, 65, 66
Blatter, Sepp, 65
Bloody Monday tradition, 39
Boca Juniors, 26, 27
Borussia Dortmund, 25, 49
Boston Game, 39
Botafogo, 27
boycotts, 32
Bradley, Michael, 41
Brazilian soccer, 9, *9*, 10, *10*, 26, *30*,
   33–34. *See also* Pelé
bribes. See match-fixing
Brooks, John, 41
Buffon, Gianluigi, 26, 35, 50, *50*, 60, 63

Cafu, 33
Cambridge University, 19, *20*
Cannavaro, Fabbio, 35
captains, 58, 59, 67
Carlos, Roberto, 33
Casillas, Iker, 50
Čech, Petr, 50
Celtic, 26
Challenge Cup, 23
Charlton, Bobby, *52*, 57, 62
Chastain, Brandi, 14, *14*
Chelsea, 47, 48, 50
Chinese soccer, 14, *14*
Clodoaldo, 9

club leagues, 24
commentators, 54
confederations, 22, *22*
Copa America Championships, 46
Copa Libertadores, 26, 27
Corinthians, 26
Crerand, Pat, 54
Crespo, Hernan, 36
Cruyff, Johan, 40, *52*, 54, *56*, 57, 62

Da Guia, Domingos, 33
danger zone, 48
Da Silva, Leonidas, 33
defenders, 49, *49*, 58–59, *59*, 63. *See also*
   specific players
dekes, 12
Del Piero, Alessandro, 35
Dempsey, Clint, 41
Didi, 33
Di Maria, Angel, 48, *48*
Di Stefano, Alfredo, *52*, 55, 62
Douglas, Jimmy, 40
Dutch soccer, 15, *15*, 26

English soccer, 11–12, *11*, *12*, 24. *See also*
   specific teams and
      players
Eredivisie, 46
Estadia Da Luz, Lisbon, Portugal, *68*
Estadio Alberto J. Armando, Buenos
   Aires, Argentina, *68*
Estadio Azteca, Mexico City, Mexico, *68*
Estadio Monumental Antonio Vespucio
Liberti, Buenos Aires,
   Argentina, *68*
Eusébio, *52*, *54*, 55, 60, 62

Facchetti, Giacinto, 35
Falcao, Radamel, 33
FC Barcelona, 25, 48
FC Santos, 27
Feabregas, Cesc, 15, *15*
Fédération Internationale de Football
Association. *See* FIFA
   (Fédération Internationale de
Football Association)
Ferguson, Alex, 61
FIFA (Fédération Internationale de
Football Association):
   berths, 65; confederations of, 22, *22*;
founding member
   countries of, 23; Goal of the Century
and, 12; Olympic
   soccer, 31; scandals, 25, 53, 65. *See*
also Women's World Cup

tournaments; World Cup tournaments
FIFA World Cup Trophy, 6, *6*
Fillol, Ubaldo, 36
Flamengo, 26
football (American), 19. *See also* Super
   Bowl XLIX
football (soccer). *See origins of soccer*
Football League Championship, 24
Football Writer's Association Footballer
   of the Year, 48
forwards, 54–55, *54*, 62. *See also specific*
      players
French soccer, 13, *13*, 26

Garrincha, 33
German soccer, 8, *8*, 25, 34–35
globalization, 65
goalkeepers, 50, *50*, 60–61, *61*, 63. *See*
also specific players
Gonsalves, Billy, 40

hacking, 19
Hamm, Mia, 32
Harvard University, 39
Hazard, Eden, 48, *48*
Henry, Thierry, 41
Hernandez, Xavi, 48
Hodge, Steve, 11
Holloway, Ian, *52*, 56
Howard, Tim, 41
Hummels, Mats, 49, *49*
Hungarian soccer, 8, *8*

Ibrahimović, Zlatan, 46
Iniesta, Andre, 15, *15*, 48
Internazionale, 26, 46
Italian soccer: about, 35; greatest
   moments, 9, 10, *10*, 13, *13*; leagues,
   25–26. *See also specific teams and*
      players

Jairzinho, 9, 33
Johnson, Ban, 40
Jules Rimet Trophy, 6
Juventus, 26, 50, 53, 56, 60

Kahn, Oliver, 35
Kaka, 41
keepers. *See* goalkeepers
kemari, *16*, 17
Kempes, Mario, 36
King Edward II, 18
King Edward III, 18
King James III, 18
King Richard II, 18

In this index, page numbers in **bold italics** font indicate photos or videos.

Klinsmann, Jurgen, 35
Klose, Miroslav, 35

LA Galaxy, 41
La Liga, 25, 49
Lampard, Frank, 41
Laporte, Aymeric, 67, *67*
Laws of the Game, *19*
Leicester City, 61
Liga BBVA, 25
Liverpool, 46, 53, 67
Lloris, Hugo, 50
London Football Association, 19
Low, Joachim, 34
ludus pilae, 17

Maier, Sepp, 35
Major League Soccer (MLS), 41
Maldini, Paolo, 35, *35*, *52*, 58, *59*, 63
Manchester United, 24, 26, 47, 48, 57, 61
The Maracana, Rio de Janeiro, Brazil, *68*
Maradona, Diego: about, 25, 36, *52*, 56, *56*, 62; greatest moments, 11–12, *11*, *12*
Marquinhos, 67
Marta, 32
match-fixing, 25, 53
Materazzi, Marco, 13, *13*
Matthäus, Lothar, 34
Meazza, Giuseppe, 35
Messi, Lionel, *24*, 25, 36, *36*, 44, *46*
midfielders, 56–57, *56*, 62
Milan, 49
"Miracle at Bern," 8, *8*, 55
mismanagement, 25
Modric, Luca, 48
Moore, Bobby, 59, *59*, 63
Muller, Gerd, 35

Napoli, 56
do Nascimento, Edson Arantes. *See* Pelé
NASL. *See* North American Soccer League (NASL)
Neuer, Manuel, 50, *50*, *75*
New York City Football Club, *41*
New York Cosmos, 27, 40
Neymar, 33–34
North American Soccer League (NASL), 27, 40. *See also* U.S. soccer

Olympic soccer, 31
origins of soccer, 17–19, 31
Orlando City Soccer Club, *41*

Paris Saint-Germain, 26, 46, 49, 67
Parma, 50
Passarella, Daniel, 36
Patenaude, Bert, 40

Pelé: about, 27–28, *27*, *28*, *52*, 54, *54*, 62; greatest moments, 9; NASL and, 40
Perez, Luis, 27
Piola, Silvio, 35
Pirlo, Andrea, 26, *26*
Platini, Michel, *52*, 56–57, *56*, 62, 65
playmakers, 48, 48, 57. *See also specific players*
Podolski, Lucas, 35
popularity of sport: international soccer, 9, 18, 23, 24, 25, 32; U.S. soccer, 41
Porto, 26
Portuguese soccer, 26
Prinz, Birgit, 32, *33*
professionalism, 23
Puskás, Ferenc, 8, *54*, 55, 62

Queen Elizabeth I, 18

Ramos, Sergio, 49, *49*
Real Madrid, 25, 26, 47, 48, 49, 55, 57
referees, 53
Ribery, Franck, 25, 47, *47*
Rimet, Jules, 31
riots, 53. *See also* violence
Riva, Luigi, 35
Rivaldo, 33
Rivelino, 9, 33
River Plate, 26
Robben, Arjen, 47, *47*, 73
Roma, 67
Romário, 33
Ronaldinho, 33, *33*
Ronaldo, Cristiano, 25, 33, *46*, 47, 55, 58, 62
Rooney, Wayne, 24, 45
Rossi, Paolo, 10, 35
rugby, 19
rules, 18–19, *19*, 39, 66
Rummenigge, Karl, 35

salaries, 24, 25, 26, 67
Santos, Djalma, 33, *52*, 59, *59*, 63
Santos, Nilton, 33
scandals, 25, 53, 65
Schalke 04, 50
Schmeichel, Peter, 61, *61*, 63
Scottish soccer, 23, 26
Seattle Sounders, 41
Seeler, Uwe, 34
Sevilla, 49
Signal Iduna Park, Dortmund, Germany, *68*
Silva, Thiago, 49, *49*
single-name players, 34. *See also specific players*
South American Leagues, 26
Spanish soccer, 15, *15*, 25

stadiums, 59, *68*
stamps, *28*
Sterling, Raheem, 67, 67
Stoke City, 61
strikers, 46, *46*. *See also specific players*
Suárez, Luis, 46
Super Bowl XLIX, 7
Swedish soccer, 46

Tostão, 33
Toure, Yaya, 48
tsu-chu, 17

UEFA, 65
U.S. soccer, 14, *14*, 27, *38*, 39–40

Valdes, Victor, 50
Vidal, Arturo, 26
violence, 20, 39, 40, 53
Voller, Rudi, 35

Walter, Fritz, 34
Wembley Stadium, 59
West German soccer, 8, *8*
West Ham United, 59
wingers, 47, *47*. *See also specific players*
Women's World Cup tournaments, 14, *14*, 32, 32, 66
World Cup tournaments: about, 7, 26; FIFA World Cup Trophy, 6, *6*; host selection process, 65–66; origins of, 31–33, 40; Pelé and, 27–28; photos and videos from, *8*, *9*, *10*, *11*, *12*, *14*, *15*, *73*; posters from, *30*, *64*

Yashin, Lev, 60, 61, *61*, 63

Zico, 33
Zidane, Zinedine, 13, *13*, 25, *52*, 57, 62
Zoff, Dino, 35, 60, *61*, 63